I0411865

HISTORIC
PUBLISHING

2015
**"Dedicated to the accurate and
Historical integrity of classic works"**

History of the African Union Methodist Protestant Church

By

Daniel James Russell

HISTORY

of the

African Union

Methodist Protestant

Church

By Right Rev. Daniel James Russell, D. D., Author.

Printed at the
Union Star Book and Job Printing and Publishing House,
131 N. Felton Street, Philadelphia, Pa.
R. S. Green, Printer.

HISTORY
of the
African Union
Methodist Protestant
Church

BY

Right Rev. Daniel James Russell, D. D., Author.

**Printed at the
Union Star Book and Job Printing and Publishing House,
131 N. Felton Street, Philadelphia, Pa.
R. S. Green, Printer.
Copyright applied for,
All rights reserved. 1920.**

HISTORY OF THE AFRICAN UNION METHODIST PROTESTANT CHURCH

By Rt. Rev. D. J. Russell, D.D., Philadelphia, Pa., Jan. 1, 1920.

PREFACE

The ministers and members of the African Union Methodist Protestant Church have anxiously watched for over one hundred years for a true history of Father Spencer and his Church--The African Union Methodist Protestant Church. A work indispensable to a proper knowledge of our origin.

The cause of our organization as a body of Methodists from the Methodist Episcopal Church.

Our established government, our progress and our present thinking.

Not only is such a work desirable among our own ministry and laity, but there are tens of thousands that are friendly to our Church who desire to have our Church history.

There are none of our 400 probationers and 20,000 members, who properly reflect upon the object, but feel that we cannot maintain our true ecclesiastical standing without a reliable history of our Church.

For the want of such a work we are frequently being misrepresented in other Church histories or Religious Encyclopedias, that get their account of our connection from unreliable sources, therefore has the author, who was born in the African Union Church and connection, seventy-four years ago, the oldest minister now living in the entire connection, under-taken the work of publishing such history. There is no branch of common literature that men attach greater importance to than history because it is the universal registry of all the known development connected with the origin and progress of our cause; it furnishes each succeeding generation of men with all the doings of the past that have come under its observation. Without it, the past of the great cycle of time would be to us and all coming time for generations, a blank.

History is properly divided into two general classes--sacred and profane.

Sacred history is divided into two branches--Biblical and Ecclesiastical.

Biblical history furnishes us with all those events connected with the origin and progress of our world necessary to be known by man, which could only be divinely given by inspired writers.

Ecclesiastical history furnishes us with the origin and progress of the various religious organizations or outgrowths of Christianity from its origin to the present.

Ecclesiastical history is necessary to note and transmit the origin, doctrines, rules and regulations developed in Christiandom that man might have full knowledge of whatever in the establishment of Sacred or Divine things would most redound to man's earthly and immortal well-being; that in the text of revealed truth, as furnished in the Scriptures. He might accept or reject religious tents. Therefore is Church History important and indispensable, it furnishes a perpetual record of the Christian Church with all its varied developments and denominational distinctions.

Church History does not only benefit the religious body, whose internal record it is, but they secure popular judgment upon religious tents and give general scope to the investigation of religious truth or error as might be disseminated by religious bodies in denominational branches of church history.

It is not the province of the historian to indulge in criticism or animadnession on the creed fundamentals of other religious sects. Under this connection in furnishing our Church History I shall aim simply to set forth facts connected with the incipient incentives to our establishing an independent religious body.

With the attendant measures, movements, success, reversions and our progressive developments for over one hundred years, it is proper that the Christian world should have some knowledge of the principles that incited us to seek separation from our white brethren and to worship by ourselves. We were actuated by pure Christian principles. We were fully conscious of certain great truths that the Bible taught., upon which our cause would be justified in the judgment of the Christian world.

8

The first great religious truth that awake our reflection and incited us to action on the subject of our own separate organization was that Christianity has provided a form of brotherly love sufficiently broad to admit all Christ's followers to full religious fellowship and religious association.

A platform so broad as to exclude the necessity of cast or race proscriptional to prevent their association as a religious brotherhood; being a religious social detriment having settled upon this great truth, we felt hesitancy in seeking to establish ourselves in an organization with a religious platform where no race proscriptions or frictions could restrict our religious privileges, enjoyments and interrupt our brotherly associations as the followers of Christ.

The second great truth taught by Christianity, another incentive to our determined purpose in establishing our separate organization, was that the Gospel of Christ intended and provided that men converted to Christianity and called into the work of the Gospel ministry; that such men had a right to and should engage in the work of evangelizing mankind irrespective of their race or cast.

Fully conscious of this great truth we feel it our privilege and our duty to put ourselves in possession to enjoy this Christian privilege.

A third essential or important truth that prompted us in our conception and purpose of separate and independent organization was that the Christian Church was a religious compact that could be organized in separate local societies under such form of local government as circumstances might dictate, and that each member of such local organization had an equal franchise in the formation of their ecclesiastical constitution or local church government. There was to us the conception in the light of Divine Truth that Christian men and women had a common Christian right to take part in legislating for their own government. To secure the advantage of this principle we were still further induced to form an independent and separate organization from the M. E. Church. To secure this great fundamental principle an inherent right in man, either in secular or religious government, we have in our ecclesiastical economy secured to layman, a representative in our legislative department, as well as in the judicial. These are some of the radical considerations that led us to determine upon the establishment of a separate or independent religious organization from the M. E. Church.

In addition to what has been given on the cause or origin of this body, the following history furnishes information as to movements, measures, success, reverses and progressive developments during over one hundred years.

Dedicated to the ministers, members and friends of the African Union Methodist Protestant Church.

Dedicated to the ministers, members and friends of the African Union Methodist Protestant Church.

By Right Rev. Daniel James Russell, D. D., Author.

In the history of civilization and in the progress of the Christian Church, this great truth has been established that in every great crisis of either church or state when the occasion required the need of a great leader there has always been some one ready and willing to lead the cause.

This was true in the history of the children of Israel after years of toil and suffering. When the time came for a Moses to lead them from the land of Egypt to the promise land a Moses came forth.

It was true also in the 16th century when the condition of the Christian Church needed a leader to start the great reformation movement, a Luther came forth. It was also true in the history of our race in this country when the time came for the overthrow of American Slavery a Lincoln came forward, and it was so too in the religious history of our people in this country when the time came for a great leader to start this great cause, a Spencer came forward. The Lord has always had a man to do his work.

The poet has truthfully said:

"The Lord is able when the occasion requires
To produce a man His work to do,
He may be humble in birth, and lowly in condition,
Yet He can make him a leader tried and true."

About the year 1779, in Kent County, Maryland, a boy child was borned, who in the Providence of the Lord, was to become the great leader in the cause of the Religious liberty of our people in this country. He was humble in birth, and surrounded with the unfavorable conditions, such as was common to our people at that time, no person who saw (at that time) that frail speck of humanity could have believed that in that humble birth was the beginning of the life of that great pioneer and Christian hero, Peter Spencer.

His early days up to manhood were passed at his birth home under the care of a slave master. This continued until the death of his master. He soon after that left his birth-place to make his home in Wilmington, Dela. Long before this in his country home the Holy Spirit had touched his heart and he had become a follower of the blessed Master. Soon after his arrival in Wilmington he connected with the Asbury M. E. Church, the so-called Mother of Methodism in the State of Delaware.

We who now live and enjoy the privilege of worshipping God under our own vine and fig-tree can scarcely conceive the conditions which then existed and the bitter experience and fiery trials our mothers and fathers at that time had to pass through in their worship and service of the Lord. The old sainted mothers and fathers who were touched by the Holy Spirit and felt to express their joy and praises to God in words aloud were made quickly to understand that they were to be seen but not heard.

This treatment Peter Spencer looked upon as being unfair to him and his people, and he did not hesitate to express his disapproval of it. This bold stand of his directed the attention of his own people to him as their leader; they looked to him for advice and counsel. He was, indeed, a race man, he believed that his people were entitled to the same religious liberties of others; too much honor can never be given him for his courage and zeal in defending his people, unborned hundreds shall yet sing his praises.

This continued spirit of restriction and ostracism was unbearable to one who possessed his independence and manly feeling. He knew that only a few years previous to that, on the 4th of July, 1776, at Independence Hall, Philadelphia, the bell of the Nation had rung out the freedom of the Nation's birth, and a part of that freedom was declared to be the constitutional right of every man to worship God in accordance to the dictates of his own conscience.

It was under such conditions and trying circumstances that the great worth of Father Spencer began to show forth. He was a born leader and in him the Lord had implanted the spirit of Christian courage, so absolutely necessary in the leadership of the Christian Church. It was with him as was with nearly all of the other great Christian leaders. He possessed not only great courage, but also great faith in God. Like Martin Luther, the great leader of the reformation movement of the 16th Century; like John Knox,

11

the great champion of the Scottish reformation; like John Wesley, the father of the great Methodist family, and many others who, like Father Spencer, were men of great courage and faith in God.

He contended for more religious liberty for himself and his people in their worship and service to God, but this was denied them. He, with his undaunted spirit and faith and trust in God, was not willing to submit longer to the conditions as then existed in the Church. In his statement of the causes which made them ask permission to build a church of their own to worship in, he said: "In the year 1805 we, the colored members of the Methodist Church in Wilmington, thought that we might have more satisfaction of mind than we then had if we were to unite together and build a house for ourselves, which we did the same year. The Lord gave us the favor and the good will of all religious denominations, and they all freely did lend us help, and by their good graces we got a house to worship the Lord in."

While preparing to build, the first separate service held by them was said to have been in a little grove between Lombard and Pine streets above Fourth, Wilmington, Del. They soon after secured a house near Fifth and French streets, where they worshipped for a little while.

The Lord greatly blessed them and they soon secured a building lot at Ninth and French streets, Wilmington, and in due time they built there the first church of their own to worship to themselves. This was all in the year 1805.

They having succeeded in getting their own church and holding separate worship, supposed they would be allowed to have some say in its business affairs. They at this time had no thought of starting a free and independent church of their own, but only wished to worship separately under the control and jurisdiction of those over them. They were told they had no rights and would not be allowed to have anything to do with the business affairs of the church. This seemed unreasonable and unfair to them how little they knew that through this treatment the Lord would so shape events out of which would come this first free and independent church of our people, bearing out in full the promise contained in Romans 8:28: "That all things work together for good to them that love the Lord and are called according to his purpose."

How true, indeed, are the words of the poet:
"God moves in a mysterious way,

His wonders to perform,
He plants his foot-steps in the sea,
And rides upon the storm."

The continued denial of being permitted to have anything to do with the business affairs Father Spencer and his followers unwillingly refused to submit to. They contended for their rights, much trouble and dissatisfaction continued, and many of them were expelled from the church and others were compelled to go to court. This contention continued until December, 1812. They were then made to understand they must submit willingly or give up the church. Those were dark days for that little band of Christian heroes; they were made to realize the forces against them were more than they could overcome; they were defeated but not discouraged, but with the same spirit that prompted the Pilgrim Fathers in the days of the colonies to leave their native homes and cross a stormy ocean of three thousand miles, so that here in the wilderness of a new world they could worship God free and undisturbed, prompted Father Spencer. He was convinced if they hoped to enjoy the God-given right of full religious liberty, they would have to organize a free and independent church of their own, and so in act he determined to obey the immortal words of Patrick Henry: "To have religious liberty or let it be religious death."

On or about the 1st of June in the year of 1813, Peter Spencer with his followers, Wm. Anderson, London Govens, John Agnes, Benjamin Webb, John James, Perry Cooper, Luke Bashten, Richard Jackson, Peter Clayton, Simon Weeks, George Hood, Jacob Collins, John Kelly, John Simmons, Lydia Hall, Susan Hicks, Ezekiel Coston, Scotland Hill, David Smith, Jacob March, Edmond Hayes, Moses Chippy, John A. Anderson, Stephen Beardly, Maggie Debbety, Philip Closs, Anna Trunn, Charles Reed, Grace Powell, Abraham Valentine, James Back, Samuel Byard, Peter Ripply, Sarah Hall, Joseph Nicholas, William Tourborn, Margaret Allen, Jacob Anderson, Joshua Young and possibly one or two others left the church they had built at Ninth and French streets, Wilmington, Del., for the purpose of starting a free and independent church of their own. How little did they know they then were about to light the torch of Religious liberty that with other torches soon then would be lighted never to be extinguished, and that within the period of one hundred years from every hill top, valley and plain in this broad land of ours the praises of our God would be ascending from hundreds, yes thousands of free and independent colored churches manned and controlled by members of their own race.

They were soon successful in securing another building lot on French street between Eighth and Ninth streets, Wilmington, and it is said they were assembled and held their first free and independent service ("a dry love feast"), on June 1st, 1813, and sang the hymn arranged by Father Spencer for this great occasion:

"Let Zion and her sons rejoice, behold the promised hour,
Her God hath heard her mourning voice and comes to exalt
His power,
It shall be known when I am dead and left on long record,
That ages yet unborned may read and trust and praise the
Lord."

I have often wondered just what was the feelings of Father Spencer and his followers that first June day, 1813, after they left their church, Ninth and French streets, without knowing just what the future had in store for them. They were like the Pilgrim Fathers in 1620, who started across the briny ocean not knowing what to expect. But like Esther of old when the judgment of death was upon her people their only hope was for her to appeal to the king, yet she knew to approach him without his bidding might mean death, but with true race devotion and without fear of death she declared, "I will go to the king if I perish, I perish." So with Father Spencer and his followers on that memorable day without fear trusting in God they started forth.

In church history we read of a Luther, a Calvin, a Knox, a Wesley and many others, but the full history of the struggles and sacrifices of the past Christian heroes will never be completed until the name of Father Spencer, too, shall have its place among the other Christian heroes of the past.

They soon after erected their first free and independent church on their lot on French street between Eighth and Ninth, Wilmington, and in keeping with the act of incorporation previously passed at Dover, Del. (and so recorded), arranged that in July, 1813, they fully organized with due forms and ceremonies, and early in September of that year (said to be the 14th) Peter Spencer was chosen and set part with full authority.

This new and independent church was legally recorded at Dover, Del., September 18, 1813, under the title of the Union Church of Africans, with the following trustees: Peter Spencer, John Kelly, John Simmons, Scotland Hill, David Smith, Jacob March and Benjamin Webb. Afterwards called the

African Union Church, since changed to our present title, the "African Union Methodist Protestant Church."

By some it has been questioned as to whether Father Spencer did really organize the first free and independent church of our people. This fact is proven beyond the shadow of doubt. Bishop Simpson in his history of Methodism, page 877, stated: "Spencer's church was organized three years before the next other independent church was organized." It is also stated in the history of the State of Delaware, page 750:

"That Peter Spencer organized the first free and independent church entirely under the control of colored people in the United States." With statements from such disinterested authorities as these quoted must establish without the possibility of successful contradiction Father Spencer's priority in his independent church and that it was indeed the first one established in the United States under the full control of our people.

We think of Washington as the Father of his Country, "first in war, first in peace and first in the hearts of his countrymen," and his memory will ever be fondly cherished by us all, and so it ought to be, for it was he who, when in the dark hours of this Nation's struggle for liberty and justice, led them safely to victory. What Washington did for this country Father Spencer did for this church. What Washington is to this country, Father Spencer is to this church, and he, too, will ever be first to his church and people in their love and devotion, for when they were struggling against discrimination and opposition, he dared to become their champion and led them safely through; as this Nation will ever fondly cherish the name and memory of Washington so this church and people will ever revere and love the name and memory of Father Spencer. Yes, it was he in the organization of this church of ours who gave the first positive evidence of our ability as a race in the independent self-government of our own religious worship, and the successful administration of our own church affairs. With all due respect for what others have done since, but it must be accredited to him the beginning of the great independent church work among our people.

Contemporary with him and only second to him in importance as one of the leaders and founders of our church was Father William Anderson. He, associated with Father Spencer in advice and council, his life ran parallel with the life of Father Spencer's. They both passed away in the year 1843.

For over one hundred years this church has stood on the shore of time unceasingly pointing men and women to the Heaven of rest. There has not been one day, no not one hour during this whole time but what the beacon light of Heaven has in some way shown forth from this church and hundreds, yes, thousands, have been safely landed over and met their loved ones on the other side.

Father Spencer, our great founder, departed this life July 25th, 1843, after thirty years of continuous and great service to his church and people, devotedly loved by his church and highly respected by the whole community. In his death our race lost one of its great champions and devoted leaders. It could have then been said of him as was said in the death of one of old: "A great man fallen in Israel to-day."

His death was the cause of great sorrow in his churches and among his people. The following is a verse of a hymn composed to his memory and was sang for many years afterward:

> "Oh, where is Father Spencer?
> I wonder where he's gone?
> The church is all in mourning,
> And he cannot be found."

"The Delaware City Gazette," a very prominent paper, in referring to his death, said: "His character, veracity and honor were without reproach. He was intelligent and dignified and exercised a wonderful influence over his people."

Over seventy years have passed since his death. More and more as we think of what he did we realize the greatness of his work. He will never be forgotten. His memory will ever be fondly cherished by this church and people 'till rolling years shall cease to move.

And as said in the Scriptures of one of old, "Being dead yet he speaketh," so we can say of Father Spencer. He yet speaketh to us through and by the great work he did for his church and people.

For he not only organized and established the church, but he also worked faithfully for the success of the church. He was the first independent missionary and church extension worker of our independent church. Think what it meant in those dark days when rejected and despised, yet he dared and did go forth and for thirty years traveled East, West, North and South, preaching, teaching and establishing free and independent churches. With the forty or more members who went forth with him was the beginning of our first church extension work. And in the years of his traveling he organized and established thirty churches. Some of us now, under the peaceful sunlight of full religious liberty, have never established one church. Yet then he was able to establish thirty.

Father Spencer's great work for his church and race was also in the fundamental principles of right and righteousness upon which he established this church. For this is true, the church was then and now is the great medium through which we reach our people, and the more perfected and secured the teaching of the church are, the more helpful they are to us as a race.

The fundamental principles established by him were first the sacredness of the home and the sanctity of the marriage vow.

He believed and taught the home above all places next to the church ought to be pure and undefiled. He believed as his church now believes that the permanent future greatness of our race depends largely upon the proper regard we as a race have for our homes. The great importance of this teaching of his must be acknowledged by all who recognize this great truth. That for any struggling race like ours battling against opposition and the baneful effects of the years of slavery we had to pass through to hope to rise to the full height of this enlightened age, great care must be exercised in the home lives, so that there might go out from them the true principles of usefulness and right.

He also strongly advocated sobriety and temperance. He knew that among the greatest foes of our race would be intemperance, and with its pangs of destruction, if we were not careful, would help to keep us down; he urged his members to refuse all intoxicants as a beverage; he likewise taught them the necessity of industry and economy, to be careful how they used their money. He himself was a living example of industry and thrift. In addition to the instruction named given by him he also urged upon them the importance of education, and instructed his people to have their children attend school. He himself was fairly well informed and knew the need of education for his people. He advised wherever they had a church for the people to try to have a school-house for the children and it was generally so arranged that such was the case. A proof of this is of the thirty churches organized by him, with few exceptions, there was a school-house connected with each one. This shows his great interest in the education of his people. It has been supposed by some that Father Spencer did not favor an educated ministry, but such was not the case. He did, but with him then, as with his church now, he believed those who preached the gospel ought to be divinely called to the work, and then to be aided by all the education they could possibly get. The following is the summary of the instructions he placed in his book of law for to guide and direct his members:

"It is expected of all who continue with us that they should continue to evidence their desire of salvation by doing no harm and avoiding evil of every kind, especially such as taking the name of the Lord in vain, profaning the day of the Lord, drinking of spiritous liquors as a beverage, fighting, quarreling, returning evil for evil, dealing in lotteries and policies, trying to take advantage in buying and selling, borrowing without a probability of paying. He also urged upon them to pay their just debts, to live decently at home, rule well their own families, to bring up their children in decency, teach them to be industrious and to be saving with their means, to avoid all needless expenses and in all things to live examplary lives."

Such was the wise instruction so recorded in 1813 and given by Father Spencer to his people. No one but a great leader with great forethought and love for his people would have thought it necessary to have so carefully and wisely instructed them. In this way he laid the foundation for these great principles of his church for all time to come. Men may come and men may go, but the great fundamentals of right and righteousness implanted by him will ever remain as the immovable landmarks of this church.

We read in the sacred Scripture, Rev. 14:13: "Blessed are the dead which die in the Lord, from henceforth: yea saith the spirit that they may rest from their labours, and their work do follow them."

By this we understand the good works of the servants of the Lord do not stop at death, but will follow on and on after they have passed. If this is true, and true it must be, because the Bible says so. What a harvest of good works have followed Father Spencer. Over seventy years has passed away since he fell asleep in death, but as the Scripture teaches, "His works are following him." Then every soul saved by this church, every life helped, every character strengthened, and every good thing done through and by this church organized by him, are the result of his good works followed him, and whatever we are or whatever we may do for the Lord, are the results of his good work following him in us.

There are many reasons why I wish to reach heaven, and among the many other reasons is, I want to see Father Spencer, and if I can I want to tell him "The old Church is moving on."

What lessons will we take from the great life and great works of our great leader, Father Spencer.

Longfellow, in that world-renowned poem of his, said:

> "Lives of great men all remind us,
> We can make our lives sublime,
> And in parting leave behind us
> Foot-prints on the sands of time."

Father Spencer in his work for the church and race has left his foot-prints on the sand of time. His foot-prints of trust and faith in God, foot-prints of zeal and courage to help the race, foot-prints of love and devotion to his church and race.

Now what will we do? This church of his comes to us as a heritage to continue the great work he began. Will we do it?

A heritage of the labors and sacrifices of our mothers and fathers, a heritage of their love and devotion to the cause of the Master. What will we do with it, this great church of Father Spencer? Will we do our part as they did theirs? If we do the day is not distant when from all over this broad land the flag of Father Spencer's church will be hoisted, and we, too, will leave our foot-prints on the sand of time.

It is not my right nor privilege to speak for others, but now on this great occasion, while the hallowed presence of our sainted father seems to pervade, and in memory of the many other sainted mothers and fathers who labored and sacrificed for us to have this church of ours, I now rededicate myself, my service, my life, and my all to this beloved church of ours. All I have belongs to it. It is mine in life, and it shall be mine in death.

QUESTIONS AND ANSWERS

Questions and answers on the history, polity and usages of the African Union Methodist Protestant Church:

Q. Who was the founder of the African Union Methodist Protestant Church?

A. Rev. Peter Spencer.

Q. When and where was he born?

A. In Kent county, Maryland, 1779.

Q. Where was he educated?

A. In a private school in Wilmington, Del.

Q. In what Church was he reared?

A. In the Methodist Episcopal Church.

Q. Where did the African Union Church begin?

A. In Wilmington, State of Delaware.

Q. When?

A. As early as 1805.

Q. Where did Father Spencer and his people worship before building their first church?

A. The first church service was held by them in a little grove on Fifth street, between Lombard and Pine streets, in Wilmington, Del,

Q. Where did they worship after leaving the grove?

A. They soon after rented a house near Fifth and French streets, Wilmington, Del., where they worshipped.

Q. What did they do after that?

A. They soon secured a building lot on the southeast corner of Ninth and French streets in the city of Wilmington, Del. There they built their first church. This was all done in A. D. 1805.

Q. Did Father Spencer and his band of followers intend to start a free and independent connection separate from the M. E. Church?

A. No. At that time they had no thought of separating from the M. E. Church and organizing a free and independent church and connection of their own.

Q. What was the cause of their separating from the M. E. Church?

A. They were told that they had no rights nor say in the selecting of a pastor, nor in the business affairs of the Church. This Father Spencer and his people considered unreasonable and unkind treatment.

Q. What happened after that?

A. After years of law suits our church and property was taken from us and we were compelled to give it up and leave it.

Q. What steps did Father Spencer then take?

A. We soon were successful in buying a lot on French street, between Eighth and Ninth streets in Wilmington, Del. Then we built the First Free and Independent Church of Colored Methodists in the United States of America and held our first meeting in it the first Sunday in June, 1813.

Q. Did the African Union Church prevail to any great extent in Father Spencer's days?

A. Yes. They organized missions, built churches and schoolhouses in Delaware, Maryland, Pennsylvania, New Jersey, New York and many other States. Many souls were converted to God: Under his direction thirty-one churches and schools were organized.

Q. When did Father Spencer die?

A. He departed this life in Wilmington, Del., July the 25th, A. D. 1843.

Q. What were his last words,

A. The battle is fought. The battle is fought and the victory is won forever.

Q. Why is the connection at times called the African Union First Colored M. P. Church?

A. On the 25th of November, A. D. 1865, a part of the First Colored Methodist Protestant Church united with the African Union Church, to be known and distinguished by the name of the African Union First Colored Methodist Protestant Church in America and elsewhere. This was done in St. Thomas F. C. M. P. Church, Baltimore, Md. God has blessed our labors.

Q. Does the African Union Methodist Protestant Church and connection recognize Bishops?

A. Yes. It was adopted by the Thirteenth General Conference, held in Chester, Pa., September, 1914.

Q. What is peculiar in the Methodist mode of ministerial supply?

A. The itineracy.

Q. What is itineracy?

A. It is the opposite of a settled pastorate. The system by which Methodist pastors are changed at stated periods.

Q. How many orders have they in the ministry?

A. Three. Deacons, Elders and Bishops.

Q. How many offices?

A. Three. That of pastor, vice president, or presiding elder, and Bishop.

Q. What does the word Bishop mean?

A. It means overseer or superintendent.

Q. Who was Father Spencer's great helpers?

A. Rev. William Anderson, Rev. Isaac Barney, Rev. Elias Saunders, Scotland Hill, David Smith, John Simons, Jacob March, John Kelley, Benjamin Webb, Rev. Edward H. Chippy, Rev. Moses Chippy and Rev. Daniel Russel, Sr., who was ordained by Father Spencer. Space will only allow us to name a few of Father Spencer's immediate helpers.

Q. What is the duty of a Bishop or president?

A. Chiefly to travel through the Connection, supervise the work, appoint the time of the annual conference, preside at them, fix the appointments of the traveling preachers, missionaries and evangelists.

Q. What is the duty of the vice president or Presiding Elder?

A Chiefly preside at the Quarterly Conference, have an oversight of the work and see that the law is strictly administered.

Q. What are the duties of a pastor?

A. Chiefly to preach the Gospel, visit the sick, bury the dead, watch over his flock, see that all of the conference claims are promptly collected and take over and enforce the Book of Discipline.

Q. What is a Missionary Bishop or president?

A. A Missionary Bishop or president's powers are restricted to a foreign field, for which he was elected and consecrated.

Q. How long can a pastor remain in one charge?

A. He may be appointed annually for an indefinite number of years.

Q. What are the leading auxiliaries in the African Union Methodist Protestant Church?

A. The Daughters of Conference, the Home and Foreign Mite Missionary Society, the Preachers' Aid Society, the A. U. M. P. Church

Building Association, the Young People's Spencer Christian League, or Christian Endeavor League, the Benevolent Club, the Sunday School Association, the Bishop's Aid Society, the Stewards' and Stewardesses and Church Extension.

Q. When does the trustees of the church make their report?

A. The trustees shall make their report regularly to the Official Board and Quarterly Conference.

GENERAL STATISTICS

General statistics of the African Union Methodist Protestant Church as reported in the late General Conference in Elkton, Md., September, 1918:

- Ministers 600
- Local preachers and Exhortors 800
- Churches 575
- Church members 20,000
- Probationers 400
- Sunday schools 850
- Officers and teachers 6,000
- Sunday school scholars 31,850
- Missions 250
- Missionaries 50
- Evangelists 25
- Institutions of learning 2

DEPARTMENTS

First--Spencer's African Union Methodist Protestant College and Seminary.

Second--Russell's Bible Training School. Established in 1904.

One publication house and book room, all located in Philadelphia, Pa. Rt. Rev. D. J. Russell, D. D., Business Manager.

We publish two monthly journals. First, the Union Star, published in Philadelphia, Pa. Established in 1882. Rt. Rev. D. J. Russell, D. D., Editor and Manager. Second, The Flash Light. Rt. Rev. J. Edward Nichols, D. D., Editor and Manager. Published in Goshen, N. Y.

Rt. Rev. John Bell, D. D., Bishop and President of the First District.

Rt. Rev. D. J. Russell, D. D., Bishop and President of the Second District.

Rt. Rev. J. Edward Nichols, D. D., Bishop and President of the Missionary District.

CHRONOLOGY OF BISHOP D. J. RUSSELL, D. D.

Son of the Rev. Daniel and Clarles Anna Russell, was born in Delaware City, Del., July 18, 1846. His father moved from the State of Delaware to Marshalltown, Salem County N. J., in 1856 His son Daniel attended the Public School in Marshalltown four years. Professor John K. Williams, Principal. He served in the late Civil War, Eleventh Regiment, Company I, United States Heavy Artillery.

1865, Honorably discharged at Camp Parpet, La. Returned home and taught Public School at Summit Bridge, Del., two years.

January 25, 1866, Converted in Mount Zion African Union Methodist Protestant Church, Marshalltown, N. J.,

1867, Called to the Ministry.

1868, Ordained to the office of a Deacon.

1870, Ordained to the office of an Elder.

May 25, 1884, Elected and ordained to the office of Bishop in the City of Wilmington, Del.

1892, Elected Editor of the Union Star, first Newspaper published by his church and connection.

1906, Elected Principal of the Bible and Training School of the African Union Methodist Protestant Church.

September 1910, Elected General Manager of the Publishing House of the African Union Methodist Protestant Church, in the Tenth General Conference, held in St. Matthew's Church, 58th and Vine Sts., Philadelphia, Pa.

1918, Pulisher of the Supplemental Bible Lessons and Catechism.

1919, Published the History of the Life of Rev. I. B. Cooper, D. D.

1920, Published the first History of the African Union Methodist Protestant Church.

We can only name a few Friends in Heaven.

REV. PETER SPENCER

Our Founder 1813.

REV. PETER SPENCER
Our Founder 1813.
AT REST

A Christian Father, Friend and Brother.

AT REST

A Christian Father, Friend and Brother.

RIGHT REV. DANIEL RUSSELL, Sr.
RIGHT REV. DANIEL RUSSELL, Sr.
Ordained by Father Spencer. President of the Middle District of the African Union Methodist Protestant Church. Past Grand Chaplain of the M. W. Hiram Grand Lodge, A. F. and A. M., of the State of Delaware. Born October 24, 1809. Departed this life April 21, 1899. "Well done, thou good and faithful servant"

REV. G. V. PETERSON, D. D., Ph D.
The Great Theologian.

REV. ISAAC BOULDEN COOPER, D. D.
Ex-General President,

RT. REV. A. W. WOODARDS, D. D.
Ex-President of the Philadelphia and New Jersey District

REV. JOHN J. HOWELL, D. D.
One of our great church workers.

REV. RICHARD BROWN, D. D.
A Preacher and a tried friend.

REV. N. F. WILSON, D. D.
Our Great Songster, one of the leading Minister's in th
Philadelphia and New Jersey District,
At Rest.

REV. N. F. WILSON, D. D.
Our Great Songster, one of the leading Minister's in the Philadelphia and
New Jersey District.
At Rest.

REV. FATHER LEWIS, D. D.
Founder of the African Union M. P. Church in Norfolk, Va.

REV. A. B. SELVEY, D. D.
Ex-Vice President of the Middle District.

REV. EDWARD CHIPPEY, D. D.
Of the African Union Church, Wilmington, Del.
First President of the District after Rev. Peter Spencer.
Died August 10, 1900.

REV. EDWARD CHIPPEY, D. D.
Of the African Union Church, Wilmington, Del.
First President of the District after Rev. Peter Spencer.
Died August 10, 1900.

MRS. SARAH JOHNS

Ex-Chairlady of the Daughters of Conference
of the Philadelphia and New Jersey District.

MRS. SARAH JOHNS
Ex-Chairlady of the Daughters of Conference of the Philadelphia and New
Jersey District.

THE LIVING PULPIT OF 1920.

RT. REV. J. H. BELL, D. D.
Bishop and President of the First District.

RT. REV. J. EDWARD NICHOLS D. D.
Bishop and President of the Missionary District.

REV. C. N. WALKER

Pastor of St. Peter's Church, W. Wilmington, Del.
President's Steward of the Middle District.

REV. J. T. RECTOR
Pastor of Chippy's Church, Hockessin, Del.
Born in Tolbert County, Md., September 11, 1873.

REV. J. T. RECTOR
Pastor of Chippy's Church, Hockessin, Del.
Born in Tolbert County, Md., September 11, 1873.

REV. J. C. DENNISON
Pastor of Star of Bethleham Church
Newport, Del.

REV. J. C. DENNISON
Pastor of Star of Bethleham Church Newport, Del.

REV. PETER BROOKINS
Presiding Elder and Vice President of the Philadelphia and New Jersey District.
15 years pastor of Mt. Zion Church, Wilmington, Del.

REV. PETER BROOKINS
Presiding Elder and Vice President of the Philadelphia and New Jersey District.
15 years pastor of Mt. Zion Church, Wilmington, Del.

REV. J. W. BROWN
Vice President of the Middle District
Pastor of the African Union Church Wilmington, Del.

REV. HENRY DAVIS
Pastor of Mount Hope African Union Methodist Protestant
Church, West Philadelphia, Pa.

REV. HENRY DAVIS
Pastor of Mount Hope African Union Methodist Protestant Church, West
Philadelphia, Pa.

Son of John Davis, Sr., was born in Queen Ann County Md., February
28, 1869. Attended Public School in the above county.

1889, Came to the State of New Jersey.

November 14, 1890, Was Converted in the A. M. E. Church,
Sweedsboro, N. J. Returned to the home of his birth and joined the M. E.
Church, in Mt. Pleasant, where father held membership for many years.

Here the Rev. Davis held office of a Class Leader and Sunday School Superintendent.

1894. He was called to preach the Gospel, was licensed as an Exhorter.

1899, Licensed a Local Preacher, came to Philadelphia, joined old Saint Matthew's African Union Methodist Protestant Church, 58th and Vine Sts. Rev. A. W. Woodards, D. D., pastor.

1912, Jonined the Annual Conference of the Philadelphia and New Jersey District.

1915, Received in the Conference by Bishop D. J. Russell, D. D.

1916, Ordained to the office of a Deacon, then to an Elder, by Bishop Russell. He was a Student in Russell's Bible Training School, Philadelphia, Pa. The Rev. Davis is a great financier and stands in the front rank of his ministerial brethren.

REV. I. H. MILLER
Pastor of Manley Chapel
Havre de Crace, Md.

REV. I. H. MILLER
Pastor of Manley Chapel Havre de Crace, Md.

REV. SIMON HINES
Pastor of New Jerusalem Church Claysville, N. J.

49

REV. G. A. COLEMAN
Pastor of Mount Plymouth Church Viola, Del.

Rev. N. F. WILSON, Jr.
One of our leading pastor's in the Phila., & N. J. District
Pastor of Saint Luke Church, Camden, N. J.

REV. GEORGE NATHANIEL SHEPPY, D. D.

REV. GEORGE NATHANIEL SHEPPY, D. D.

Born in the Island of Jamaica, April 17, 1857. Graduated from the Gurnup Mt. Seminary in 1874, Became Professor of English Literature at the following Institution. Barneyside in the Parish of Westmoreland, Green Island Gurnup Mount Little London. Landed in Philadelphia, May 1895. Joined the annual Conference of the A. U. M. P. Church at Norristown, Pa., May 1897. Ordained Elder in the A. U. Church, Wilmington, Del., May 1900. He held the office of Staticion for 19 years. Present pastorage St. John A. U. M. P. Church, Chester, Pa.

REV. MRS. LYDIA ARCHIE
The Oldest Ordained Female Preacher in the African Union M. P. Church
Chadds Ford, Pa.

THE LIVING CHURCH OF 1920

MRS. S. A. WOODARDS
President of the Home Mite Missionary Society of the
Philadelphia and New Jersey District.

MRS. S. A. WOODARDS
President of the Home Mite Missionary Society of the Philadelphia and
New Jersey District.

MRS. ELLEN RUSSELL

Vice President of the Home Mite Missionary Society of the Philadelphia and New Jersey District.

MRS. ELLEN RUSSELL
Vice President of the Home Mite Missionary Society of the Philadelphia
and New Jersey District.

MRS. MARGARET ANNA HILL
Grand Secretary of the Home Mite Missionary
of the Philadelphia and New Jersey District.
Philadelphia, Pa.

MRS. MARGARET ANNA HILL
Grand Secretary of the Home Mite Missionary of the Philadelphia and New
Jersey District.
Philadelphia, Pa.

MRS. MARY A. HENRY
Grand Secretary of the Daughters of Conference
of the Philadelphia and New Jersey District
Salem, N. J.

MRS. MARY A. HENRY
Grand Secretary of the Daughters of Conference of the Philadelphia and
New Jersey District
Salem, N. J.

MRS. S. E. RIGGS
Musical Directress at Russell's Mission, Phila., Pa.

MRS. S. E. RIGGS
Musical Directress at Russell's Mission, Phila., Pa.

REV. WILLIAM A. BROWN, D. D.
Pastor of St. John's Church, Chatham, Ontario, Canada.

REV. WILLIAM A. BROWN, D. D.
Pastor of St. John's Church, Chatham, Ontario, Canada.

ST. JOHN'S AFRICAN UNION M. P. CHURCH
Chatham, Ontario, Canada.
Built by the Rev. S. W. Chippey, D. D.
Rev. W. A. Brown, present Pastor 1920.

EBENEZER AFRICAN UNION M. P. CHURCH
Norristown, Pa.
Rev. S. W. Chippey, D. D., one of our young bright stars present Pastor
1920.

THE GRAND BODY OF THE DAUGHTERS OF CONFERENCE.
of the Philadelphia and New Jersey District.

THE GRAND BODY OF THE DAUGHTERS OF CONFERENCE.
of the Philadelphia and New Jersey District,

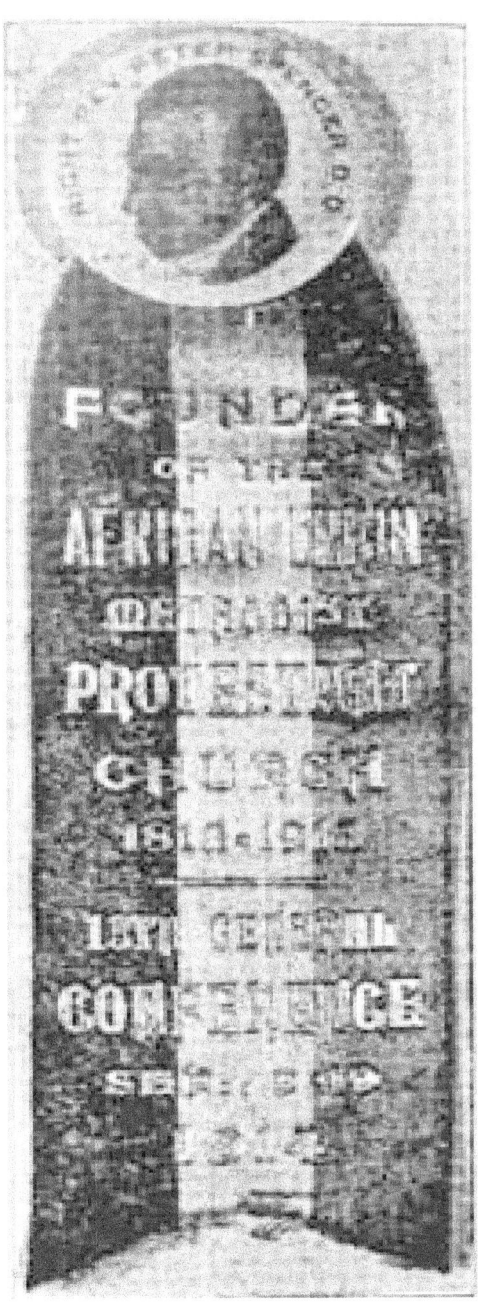

[Badge]

This cut represents the badge wore in the 13th General Conference held in St. John African Union Methodist Protestant Church, Chester, Pa. From

September 9, to 19, 1914. This General Conference adopted the title of Bishop, or Bishops to the presiding officer, or officers presiding over a dioses, or district of the African Union Methodist Protestant Church. This is a true saying, "If a man desireth the office of a bishop he desireth a good wook." 1st Timothy, 3rd Chapter, 1st verse.

OLD ST. MATTHEW'S AFRICAN UNION M. P. CHURCH
58th & Vine Sts. Philadelphia, Pa.
Built by Rev. Thomas B. Scott, D. D., in 1877.
Rebuilt by Rev. D. J. Russell, D. D., in 1909.

DIRECTORY OF EX-PRESIDENTS

Up to the change of title from President to Bishop in 1914.

- 1 Rev. Peter Spencer, Wilmington, Del. . . . . .
- 2 Rev. Edward H. Chippey, D. D., Wilmington, Del. . . . . .
- 3 Rev. Moses Chippey, D. D., Wilmington, Del. . . . . .
- 4 Rev. Benjamin Scott, D. D., Wilmington, Del. . . . . .
- 5 Rev. Daniel Russell Sr., D. D., Wilmington, Del. . . . . .
- 6 Rev. G. V. Peterson, D. D., Ph. D., Elmira, N. Y. . . . . .
- 7 Rev. John H. Nichols, D. D., Philadelphia, Pa. . . . . .
- 8 Rev. C. S. Temple, D. D., Chester, Pa. . . . . .
- 9 Rev. Isaac Boulden Cooper, D. D., Salem, N. J. . . . . .
- 10 Rev. James E. Sargent, D. D., Norristown, Pa. . . . . .
- 11 Rev. Robert H. Potts, D. D., Phila. Pa. . . . . .
- 12 Rev. George W. Brown, D. D., Wilmington, Del. . . . . .
- 13 Rev. Father Lewis, D. D., Norfolk, Va. . . . . .
- 14 Rev. C. W. Sides, D. D., Towson, Md. . . . . .
- 15 P. E. Robinson, D. D., Baltimore, Md. . . . . .
- 16 Rev. A. W. Woodards, D. D., Philadelphia, Pa. . . . . .

Ex-Vice Presidents of the Phila. & N. J. District.

- Rev. George H. Tilghman, D. D., Viola, Del. . . . . .
- Rev. James M. K. Johnson, D. D., Merchantville, N. J. . . . . .
- Rev. N. F. Wilson Sr., D. D., Salem, N. J. . . . . .
- Rev. John A. Mattee, West Fenwick, N. J. . . . . .

There are others in various districts that we have no special record of.

INDEX

This History is Composed by Bishop D. J. Russell, D. D.
Printed at the
Union Star Book and Job Printing and Publishing House,
131 N. Felton Street, Philadelphia, Pa.

by
R. S. Green, Printer.

January 1920.

CORPORAL DANIEL WEBSTER RUSSELL

The above etching represents Daniel Webster Russell, a Corporal in Battery D, 350th United States Field Artillery, Camp

CORPORAL DANIEL WEBSTER RUSSELL
The above etching represents Daniel Webster Russell, a Corporal in Battery D, 350th United States Field Artillery, Camp Dix, N. J. Suffered in severe battles over sea, in the world's war. He returned home safe, Corporal

Russell is the only son of Bishop D. J. Russell, D. D., presiding officer of the Philadelphia and New Jersey Conference. Corporal Russell is Secretary of the Conference. He was born January 20, 1895, at 107 North Felton Street, Philadelphia, Pa. Now resides in Bayonne, N. J. Corporal Russell's father is a veteran of the late civil war.

MOUNT ZION

The Mt. Zion African Union Methodist Protestant Church, Marshalltown, Salem County N. J., is the Mother Church of the Philadelphia and New Jersey District., and one of the oldest and leading churches in the connection. Rt. Rev. Isaac Boulden Cooper, D. D., our late general president; Bishop Daniel James Russell, D. D., our present presiding officer of the Philadelphia and New Jersey District; Rev. N. F. Wilson, Sr., that has crossed the swelling flood; Rev. Nathan F. Wilson, Jr., these great men was converted and started on their Christian journey from this historical church. The Rev. Henry T. Miller is the present pastor, 1920.